Bitcoin, Blockchain and Cryptocurrency Dictionary and Slang Terminology

By Javier Jerez-López

ISBN: 978-1-948656-00-9

Published by
Jerez Publishing and Arts
PO Box 141025 Arecibo
Puerto Rico 00614
jerezarts@gmail.com
www.jerez-art.com

INDEX

INDEX

INDEX

INDEX

INDEX

INDEX

INTRODUCTION

Throughout the history of the known world, every generation has had their own invention or concept that revolutionizes the way people think and interact with each other. When talking about this, inventions like: the cellphone, the internet and paper money come to mind but simple things like the wheel or a fork are also technologies that help us achieve our "normal" daily tasks. Think about it, there are things that we use in our daily lives that we truly couldn't live without or that will prevent us from accomplishing simple everyday responsibilities. Yes, you can walk anywhere you want but can you imagine yourself going to work or the supermarket without a bicycle, car or bus? Remember having to write an essay by hand and not having a computer or a printer to print your work? How about heating or cooking your food without a stove or microwave? Some of the examples are trivial concepts but you get the idea, we depend on many things and/or technological advances to complete our routines.

Even if you go camping, where most of our comforts are restricted, we still depend on many things to survive. So, is this bad? Should we feel ashamed of what we are? I don't think so, is our human condition. Humans are one of the most complex animals in existence but without the help of other humans or previously invented tools, we would die hours after being born. Humans depend on other humans and on many things to survive and that is a fact. Birds are born with wings to fly, bears have claws to hunt and humans, besides opposable thumbs, have a highly developed brain to think and create but it takes a lot of time to prepare ourselves and to mature. We "dominate" planet earth because we can think and create better than any other animal in the world. Humans are capable of creating beautiful concepts and ideas and the more we create the more efficient we become. The knowledge we accumulate as a collective helps us prepare better for the future. Every invention that we have created constantly evolves. Every year we have a different model of car, more efficient and safer. Computers get better over time, faster processors, more memory and easier to understand. But what about money? Is money developing fast enough to comply with our needs? Are your grandparents now using a different system to pay for groceries that the one that they used in the 1930s or 1940s? So why is our banking or money system progressing so slowly? The answer to the question is: our money system is not developing slowly, in fact today we have one of the most progressive, safe and versatile systems of payment that we could have ever imagined and its name is Cryptocurrency.

In order to talk about Cryptocurrency, we need to have a short but concise review of what money is and why we need it. The world revolves around money and assets. If we want to have a decent life or any kind of life for that matter, we need money. I go salsa dancing on weekends, but I can't pay my phone bill by shaking my ass, you need money for that. We need money for rent, clothes, food and every other thing you can imagine. Except for spoiled brats, we need to work for money, so money is somewhat of a price or compensation for doing something or having achieved something. Believe it or not it didn't always used to be like this. The exact place or time of the invention of money is not precisely known but for what history can gather we know this: there is recorded history of as far as 9000BC where a barter system was established. A barter system is a system in which people of a certain region exchange goods for services or other goods in order to have what is necessary for their survival. As early humans began to raise domestic livestock and cultivate plants, a system was needed to exchange stuff for stuff you didn't have, and bartering complied with everything necessary for this to happen. The value of bartering items was negotiated between each party involved in the transaction. If a farmer had chickens but needed milk he/she could trade 10 chickens for one cow and so on. One of the earliest forms of barter included chickens, cattle, vegetables, sheep and grain.

Professions like doctors and veterinarians that took care of the people and the animals and as a reward they got paid with chickens, tools and milk. Any exchange was legal and they only needed to establish their rules to process the exchange without having a third-party member supervising the transaction. Recorded history shows how the ancient empires of Egypt, China and Babylon used to have big warehouses in which employees could claim goods for their work using a coupon or claim ticket and other barns in which they traded their gains for other goods needed. Later the exchange of precious metals and materials such as gold, silver and bronze, used mostly by Romans, became a trading commodity. The system worked for many centuries and evolved, having rules and penalties. The first known currency was created in Lydia, now part of Turkey around 600BC by King Alyattes. Paper money was first established during the Tang Dynasty in China in 618-907 AD almost 500 years before it was used in Europe. Around 1150 AD the order known as The Knights Templar established a kind of travelers check in which people were issued a letter or receipt that worked as a promise of payment. The issued ticket could be cashed in at Templar Houses or lodges. The Knights Templar charged a "transaction fee" to either the lender, the borrower or sometimes both. After that paper money became very popular around the world. The governments developed a system in which people, instead of carrying coins or gold around, had some type of paper money that was backed by the amount of gold they had saved in the government's vaults. From there we have the first credit card appearing around 1946 and most recently platforms like PayPal and Ipay that let you pay wirelessly using your own paper money that was previously deposited in your bank or a credit line. So, as you can see, money as we know it, has evolved around the years but do we actually have a good, practical and fair system? Some might say it is a convenient system but having to pay insanely large amounts of money to banks just to move your money seems a little unfair. What if you want to send money around the world, let's say you want to send $5,000 from London to the United States, is this an easy thing to do? In exchange fees and transaction fees you could end up paying even as high as 20% of the amount sent. Does this seem fair? I mean we are actually just subtracting a number from an account in a computer and adding it to another account so why such high fees? Why can't I just take my money and electronically send it to my cousin how and when I want without having to pay such steep prices? Like mentioned before, there is an actual way to do all this and keep the control of what you do with your money and that system is called cryptocurrency.

In 2009 a person, group or entity using the name, Satoshi Nakamoto created the first currency for use in a peer-to-peer online transaction system and called it Bitcoin. Bitcoin is the most prominent of a group of virtual currencies or Cryptocurrencies that exists mainly as computer code and that has no central issuing authority (decentralized). Bitcoin and all Cryptocurrencies are not backed by any bank or government and can be used by anyone that can have access to a computer. Unlike other forms of digital currency, Bitcoin is truly untraceable and is mainly used to trade or purchase anything from any part of the world without having a third-party member earning fees from your transactions, so in other words you are in control of your money, and you decide what to do with it and how to do it. The idea of Cryptocurrency was created to satisfy the necessity of having some type of electronic goods or form of payment, independent from the banking system, that will allow customers and people to exchange and/or pay for things without the need of having a third person or entity charging a percent for transaction. The vast majority of Cryptocurrencies operate as a decentralized unit independently of a central bank or physical building although some banks and organizations are now building their own cryptocurrency to compete with the already established phenomenon.

When you start something new, the first thing you should always do is, take time to learn the rules, that is of course if you want to have success. One of the most important things in every new adventure is to learn the language. If you don't know what you are talking about you will never do it right. This "Bitcoin, Blockchain and Cryptocurrency Dictionary and Slang Terminology" is a guide prepared with the most important concepts you need to know about the cryptocurrency world and virtual money. It has formal concepts like: Algorithms, Hashrate and Arbitrage and more secular terms like: Hodl, Newbie and Shitcoin, both which are used in the cryptocurrency world and will give you all the necessary tools to go against the best in the business and understand what you are doing. If you are new to the crypto world or if you already have some experience working with cryptocurrency this guide will help you stay on track of the most recent terms and explain some concepts that you might not understand completely. Keep this book around you at all times. I can assure you that on more than one occasion you will have to make reference to it. Like anything you do in life, enjoy this new journey and prepare yourself, you will either have a lot of success or will crumble in defeat, but it all depends on you. Be smart and learn as much as you can, the more you learn the better you will become, good luck!

Bitcoin, Blockchain and Cryptocurrency

Dictionary and Slang Terminology

VOCABULARY

Addresses: Cryptocurrency addresses are a sequence of alphanumeric symbols used to receive and send transactions on a specific network. This identifier can also be represented as a QR code to facilitate the transaction.

Agreement ledgers: Agreement ledgers are a type of distributed ledgers used by two or more people and/or parties to negotiate and reach an agreement.

Algorithm: Algorithms are complex methods, similar to equations, used for solving a mathematical problem in a predetermined number of steps that commonly involves different types of mathematical operations. It can also be described as a step-by-step process for solving a problem usually performed by a computer program.

Altcoin: The word altcoin is an abbreviation of "Bitcoin Alternative Coin or Alternative Cryptocurrency". The vast majority of the altcoins in existence are forks of Bitcoin, most recently forks of Ethereum, with minor changes to the proof of work algorithm of the original Blockchain.

Apocalypse Block: The Apocalypse Block is the very last block in a Blockchain. When this AB is halved the price of the cryptocurrency stays as standard until further development or market corrections. Think of it as the last piece of gold mined from Earth.

Arbitrage: The concept of arbitrage is the action of buying and/or selling on different exchanges to earn the difference in the spread as a profit. The price of the cryptocurrency varies due to popularity, differences in exchange reputation, community coin preferences and ease of bank funding.

ASIC: The acronym ASIC stands for "Application Specific Integrated Circuit". The ASIC is a chip specifically customized for a particular assignment, think of it as the evolution of development after CPUs, GPUs and FPGAs. In the case of bitcoin, ASIC is intended to process SHA-256 hashing problems to mine new bitcoins.

Attestation Ledger: An Attestation Ledger is a distributed ledger that provides long lasting records of agreements, providing evidence that these statements were made. Is basically a receipt of purchase.

ATH: ATH is an acronym for "All-Time High" meaning that this specific cryptocurrency has reached its highest historical price.

ATL: ATL is the opposite of ATH, an acronym for "All-Time Low" meaning that this specific cryptocurrency has reached its lowest historical price (not very common after its ICO).

Bag Holder: Bag Holder is a term used as an insult to a trader or holder who bought a specific cryptocurrency at a high price and missed his opportunity to sell, leaving him with worthless coins. It's also used to describe holders that no matter how bad their coin is, he or she decides to keep it in hopes that someday it will become something of value.

Bitcoin: Bitcoin or BTC is what started it all. Bitcoin is the first digital currency created for use in peer-to-peer online transactions. It was introduced (first block hashed) at the beginning of 2009 by a person, group or entity using the name, Satoshi Nakamoto. Bitcoin is the most prominent of a group of virtual currencies that exists mainly as computer code and that has no central issuing authority (decentralized).

Bitcoin is not backed by any government, or asset and has a fluctuating value linked in part to a scarcity that is mathematically predetermined. Unlike other forms of digital currency, Bitcoin is truly untraceable and therefore, like cash, cannot be recovered if lost or destroyed. Bitcoin is also the main currency used to trade or purchase other altcoins in a determined exchange.

bitcoin (in lowercase):bitcoin, in lowercase, is used mostly to describe bitcoin as a unit of account, in other words, the currency, for example: "I just sent two bitcoins to your account."

Bitcoin Cash: Bitcoin Cash or BCH is a hard fork of Bitcoin created in 2017. Some miners and investors had several debates and discrepancies with the Bitcoin Blockchain and in August of 2017 a new bitcoin Blockchain was created. (See Bitcoin and Hard Fork)

Block Height: The Block Height is the number of blocks in the chain between it and the genesis block. The Genesis Block has a height of 0. One way to find the correct value could be taking the length of the chain and subtracting the Genesis Block.

Block Reward: A Block Regard is the incentive given to a miner that has successfully hashed a transaction block. Block rewards are based on the rules used by the cryptocurrency and they are calculated using the cost of the transaction fees and coins. Each cryptocurrency has a predetermined reward, in the case of Bitcoin, it was established from its creation and this cannot be changed without agreement between the entire Bitcoin network. The Bitcoin block reward started at 50 BTC in the Genesis Block (block #1) and halves every 210,000 blocks. This will continue until block 210,000, from block 210,001 on, the rewards will be 25BTC. Since blocks are mined on average every 10 minutes, 144 blocks are mined per day. At 144 blocks per day, 210,000 blocks take on average four years to mine.

Blockchain: The Blockchain is what really backs up all cryptocurrencies. Think of it as a giant spider web entangling many computers around the world on a specific task. Is an innovative technology that works as a type of distributed ledger that consist of unchangeable, digitally recorded information in packages called blocks where each of this blocks are linked to the next block using a cryptographic signature permitting block chains to be used like a ledger, which can be shared and retrieved by anyone with the appropriate authorization (see Cryptocurrency and Satoshi Nakamoto).

Block Ciphers: Block Ciphers are a technique of encrypting text generating a cipher-text in which a cryptographic key and algorithm are applied to a block of data all together as a group, at once, as a group instead of one bit at a time.

Borrowing Rate: Borrowing Rate is a kind of interest based on the cryptocurrency that you borrow and established at a predetermined rate.

BTFD: BTFD is an acronym of the slang phrase "Buy the Fucking Dip". It usually refers to a cryptocurrency whose price drops drastically and in hopes that the specific cryptocurrency increases in value you are advised to buy.

Butthurt: This slang term describes a cryptocurrency trader or holder that makes a bad move or trade, and his/her cryptocurrency drops drastically.

Buy and Sell Wall: The Buy and Sell walls is a situation created either by the popularity of a cryptocurrency, or it can also be infused by a group or a Whale to manipulate the market.

This usually occurs when a group or one buyer with a big order, limits the price of a specific cryptocurrency with his/her purchase, for example: let's invent a cryptocurrency called Jerezcoin. Say you want to buy 20 units of Jerezcoin, that trades for $2, but you only want to pay $1 for each one (you want to pay $20 instead of $40). What you do is, place an order that will become activated once the price reaches $1. Now let's just say that I don't want the price of Jerezcoin to drop to $1, so what I do is create a Wall placing a larger order, I place an order of 20,000 Jerezcoins at $2 so that in order for the price of Jerezcoin to drop below $2 my order must be completed first effectively blocking the price of Jerezcoin from dropping.

Buy the dip: is a slang phrase meaning "buy now that the price is low". Unexperienced buyers tend to sell once the market goes down because of FUD costing them lots of money. More experienced traders buy when it's down and sell when it's high. (See Dip and Weak Hands)

Central ledger: The Central Ledger refers to a ledger maintained by a centralized organization.

Chain linking: The Chain Linking is a special type of process in which two Blockchains are connected with each other with the purpose of chain-to-chain transaction permitting transaction and exchanges with sidechains

Cipher: A Cipher is the algorithm used for performing the encryption or decryption of information.

Circulating Supply: The Circulating Supply is the number of coins that are circulating in the market and in the general public's hands.

Classic: Classic is a common name or classification used to describe something related to cryptocurrency that has been around since or near the beginning. In some cases, the name can be used in a fork to differentiate the newly created cryptocurrency from the old one such as: Ethereum Classic or Bitcoin.

Coin: A coin is a cryptocurrency that can operate independently on its own (see Token).

Confirmation: Confirmation is the answer or answers you get when a Blockchain transaction has been verified by the network. It can also be seen as an alphanumeric code. It works the same way as a receipt, and It also gives you the confidence that your transaction was successful.

CPU/GPU Mining: CPU and GPU stand for "Central Processing Unit and Graphical Processing Unit" and it basically describes the act of mining with your computer. This is the least powerful classification of bitcoin mining hardware that you can have. The amount of money you need to pay for electricity compared to the amount of BTC you get is not proportional and tends to be counterproductive. Theoretically you could enhance your bitcoin hash rate by adding graphics hardware to your desktop computer so that your computer can calculate complex mathematical algorithms faster, but the pricing tends to be very high. (See Mining)

Cryptanalysis: Cryptanalysis is the ability to decipher coded messages or enigmas without having the key or legend.

Cryptocurrency: Cryptocurrency is an encrypted digital currency (as the name suggests) based on mathematical algorithms, attached to a Blockchain technology and where encryption procedures are used to regulate the generation and transmission of currency while allowing a process of verifying the funds transfer. The idea of Cryptocurrency was created to satisfy the necessity of having some type of electronic goods or form of payment, independent from the banking system, that will allow custumers and people to exchange and/or pay for things without the need of having a third person or entity charging a percent for transaction. The vast majority of Cryptocurrencies operate as a decentralized unit independently of a central bank or physical building (see Blockchain and Satoshi Nakamoto).

Cryptography: This concept refers to the process of encrypting and decrypting information.

Dapp: Also D-App, is an abbreviation of "Decentralized Application". It's basically an app that has its core code and/or programming running on a decentralized Blockchain network.

DAO: DAO is an acronym for "Decentralized Autonomous Organization", basically an organization working on a Blockchain without human control.

DDOS: DDOS is an acronym for "Distributed Denial of Service". It occurs when a computer network stops orders and won't sell/trade or as an intentional paralyzing of a computer network by saturating it with data sent concurrently from many computers or systems permitting only pre-established orders.

Decryption: Decryption is the process of transforming encrypted or coded data to readable or understandable text format.

Digital Commodity: A Digital Commodity is an electronic good or currency, viewed as a code or a number, specially designed to move, trade or purchase using the internet and that usually leads to profit margins.

Digital Identity: A Digital Identity is an online coded and unique identification tool adopted in the World Wide Web, usually used to locate or identify someone. The information contained in a digital identity allows authentication of a user interacting with a business system on the web without the involvement of human connection.

Distributed Ledger: A Distributed Ledger is a transaction databank, spread across the Blockchain network around the world. All transaction information is stored one after the other in a continuous record.

Difficulty: Difficulty, although used in many situations in the cryptocurrency world, is used specifically to denote how hard it is to verify blocks in a Blockchain network. The difficulty of mining adjusts verifying blocks every 2016 blocks.

Dip: A Dip in Cryptocurrency refers to a drop in price. (See Buy the Dip and Weak Hands)

Double Spend: A Double Spend refers to a situation in which a person tries to send a cryptocurrency transaction to two different addressees at the same time either by mistake or trying to confuse the system to see if they can bank double the amount.

Encryption: Encryption is the process of transforming readable or understandable text into encrypted or coded format.

Ether: Ether is the token of the Ethereum Blockchain. Its functionality is based on the exchange reward for transaction fees, miner rewards and other services on the network.

Ethereum: Ethereum is a decentralized software platform based on Blockchain technology, and inspired by bitcoin, that enables developers to write smart contracts and applications that run exactly as programmed without any possibility of downtime, censorship, fraud or third-party interference (no bank or centralized organization to earn a percentage). The platform was created by a Russian programmer by the name of Vitalik Buterin.

Ethereum Classic: ETC was created because the Ethereum platform was forked into two versions: "Ethereum" (ETH) and "Ethereum Classic" (ETC). After the hard fork, the new tokens were named Ethereum, and the original version were renamed Ethereum Classic. Ethereum Classic appeared as the result of disagreement with Ethereum regarding the DAO Hard Fork (See Ethereum and Hard Fork).

Exodus Block: The Exodus Block is the name given to the second block on a Blockchain.

Fiat currency: Fiat Currency is basically a determined currency declared legal by a government to be used in that specific country or region. Before, money was backed up by the amount of gold that that determined country had, today, the value of fiat money is derived by the capacity of that government to pay and the faith people have in the capacity of the country.

Fill or Kill: A fill or kill is the name used to describe a limit order that will not take effect unless an opposite order exceeds this limit order's quantity.

FOMO: FOMO is an acronym for "fear of missing out". The term is mostly used to denote the act of buying induced by fear.

Fork: A fork occurs when a miner takes a copy of the source code and starts developing it for "solutions" to a problem or to make it better, creating an evolved piece of software (for some good, for some irrelevant). Think of it as two miners finding an effective hash coming up with an operational solution to solve the problem. The miner/s promote the change for verification to their miner group

If accepted, usually, the network will split into two branches, where one half of the network stays with the current version (old or classic version) of the block while the other half of the network believes in a different block (solution).

FUD: FUD is the acronym for "fear, uncertainty and doubt", another term used by people or groups to manipulate the market.

Full node: A Full Node is a computer that completely puts into effect all of the rules of the Blockchain.

(See: Node).

Genesis Block: The Genesis Block is the very first block in a Blockchain.

Halving: The Term Halving is used to describe the action of adding a new block to the Blockchain. When this event occurs the miners are rewarded with Bitcoin for their work. (See Mining and Proof of Work)

Hardfork: A Hardfork is a permanent division or divergence of a specific Blockchain that creates two simultaneous branches, with a base of the original data and history. This Hardfork creates two parallel Blockchains, one with the original rules and protocols and the other one with the new, predetermined changes established by the miners, in hopes of improving the Blockchain. It is not backwards compatible (the software rejects all transactions from the older software versions) and every miner running nodes in the network would need to upgrade to their new software to recognize new blocks. Examples of Hard forks: Bitcoin Classic, Bitcoin Gold and Bitcoin Cash (Note: some people don't recognize them as such). (See Softfork and Source Code Forks)

Hashrate: Hashrate is the number of hashes that can be achieved by a miner in a specified interval of time.

Holder: The term Holder usually refers to a cryptocurrency enthusiast that instead of trading his/her cryptocurrency, holds it, in hopes that in the future its price will increase.

HODL: The concept of HODL is not an actual concept but a misspelling of the word 'hold' that stuck around to mean 'keep'. A crypto trader who buys a coin and does not see himself selling in the foreseeable future is called a hodler of the coin (holder can also be used). Most recently it also has been interpreted as an acronym for "Hold On for Dear Life".

Initial Coin Offering: An ICO is an event in which a new cryptocurrency sells tokens in advance in exchange for upfront capital to develop its idea.

Key: In the world of Cryptocurrency, a Key is an alphanumeric code that can also be represented as a QR Code, basically a secret code to access something crypto related. (See Private Key and Wallet)

Ledger: A Ledger is a database where every transaction of a cryptocurrency is recorded, kind of like a digital record. The Bitcoin Blockchain is a global ledger where all transactions of bitcoin that have ever happened are recorded. The complete ledger is downloadable.

Lending Rate: The Lending rates are used by some exchanges that have lending accounts. In these exchanges you can deposit your cryptocurrency to lend your coins for others to trade. The lending rate fluctuates throughout the day based on the demand, popularity and amount deposited.

Limit Order: A Limit Order in a buy/trade option or order that can be placed on an exchange at a future price that will execute when the price target is met.

Litecoin: Litecoin is a peer-to-peer cryptocurrency that enables instant, near-zero cost payments to anyone in the world without the involvement of a third party. It was created in 2011 by Charlie Lee, a former Google and Coinbase employee. The Litecoin network went live on October 13, 2011. It was a fork of Bitcoin rather than a Source Code Fork. LTC has the advantages of having a decreased block generation time, increased maximum number of coins and a different hashing algorithm (scrypt instead of SHA-256). With substantial industry support, trade volume and liquidity, Litecoin is a proven medium of commerce complementary to Bitcoin. In a world where houses will be bought with BTC and cars with ETH, Litecoin could very well be a day-to-day currency.

Market Capitalization: The Market Cap in the cryptocurrency market, is used to illustrate a coin's supremacy over others. It's calculated by multiplying the Price by the Circulating Supply, {MC = P X CS}.

Max Supply: The Max Supply of a cryptocurrency is the best approximation of the maximum amount of coins that will ever exist of that specific cryptocurrency.

Mining: Mining is the method by which transactions are verified and then added to a Blockchain in what we call halving, when this event occurs the miners are rewarded with Bitcoin (on the Bitcoin Blockchain) for their work. To get a clear view, mining is just a bunch of computers solving cryptographic problems/transactions using computing power from around many computers or nodes around the world linked together for that unique purpose, in a sense this is a very easy and normal problem to solve. The process of Bitcoin mining consumes a lot of computational power and electrical energy to solve the mathematical problems and transactions; it consumes so much energy that it is estimated that one Bitcoin transaction requires the amount of electrical energy needed to fully power 1.5 American households daily. (See Proof of Work and Halving)

Multi-signature: Multi Signature or multisig are the collection of addresses (two or more) that allow multiple parties to require more than one key to authorize a transaction. This is mostly done with companies so that no one person can control the flow of the currency. The amount of signatures needed is decided in the formation process or construction of the address. This is also a great way to protect your currency.

Newbie or Noobs: Another slang concept utilized very often is Newbie or Noobs, this refers to a recent investor, cryptocurrency trader or holder, the new guy, usually viewed as inexperienced and an easy target.

Node: A node is no other than a computer, any computer that connects to the Blockchain network (See: Full node).

Off Ledger Currency: Off ledger currencies are currencies that can be used with a digital wallet but weren't created for a specific digital wallet, this includes: the US Dollar and the Euro, to name a few, that can be sent to a digital wallet for online purchases but where in fact created for capital management and purchase stuff in a specific country or region.

On-Ledger Currency: An On Ledger currency is a currency issued on ledger that has the fundamental purpose of using it on ledger. An example of this would be Ethereum and Bitcoin.

Peer: A peer is a person or entity involved in a cryptocurrency transaction. Peer can also be used to describe a person, a group of computer programs that shares responsibility for maintaining the uniqueness and integrity of the ledger and transactions.

Peer-to-peer: Peer to peer or (P2P) refers to a transaction between two people, groups or entities in a specific network without the necessity of having a third party, such as banks, involved in the negotiation.

Permissioned ledger: A permissioned ledger is a ledger where the owner or actors must have certain rights to access or contribute to the ledger. When new information is added the ledger is verified in a consensus process in one or many places around the world.

Permissioned Blockchains: Permissioned Blockchains are Blockchains created with an access control layer into their nodes that permits and restricts actors from participating in the consensus mechanism of the blockchain's network.

Private Currency: A private currency is a particular legal tender, issued by a reserved group, company or person typically secured against uninsured resources. A Private currency can be created by anyone and can be worth as much as that person wants depending on what is backing the currency.

Private Key: A Private Key is an alphanumeric combination or QR Code that contains the only means of access to your account, besides your username and password. With this code you can access your private wallet or recover your wallet from any computer. This Private Key is never to be given to anyone and there's no way to recover it once it's lost.

(See Key and Wallet)

Proof of Authority: Put in simple words, Proof of Authority or POA is an algorithm or modification of the POS algorithm that instead of using a stake with a monetary value, the identity of the validator serves as stake (people will and need to know who you are).

There's been a lot of criticism due to the fact that one of the main reasons cryptocurrency was created was anonymity but at the same time many traders feel safe knowing that the person who handles the mining is known, has to have an approved account as a validator and a personal identification with legitimately issued certification or documentation. The POA awards a certain reputation to the account or validator guaranteeing that the validator will uphold the transaction so that they don't get a negative reputation, kind of like eBay, do a good job and you get stars and a good standing. (See Proof of Work and Proof of Stake)

Proof of Stake: Proof of Stake or POS is an alternative method, for creating blocks on the Blockchain, to the proof of work system that, in a sense, seeks to address the issue of energy consumption and reduce risk of centralization while maintaining its capabilities and secureness.

Contrary to the POW the POS is a consensus algorithms for public Blockchains that depend on a validator's economic “stake” in the network, this means that the amount of that currency that you hold, is used to calculate the amount of that currency that you can mine. In POS a group of validators take turns proposing and voting on the next block. The weight of each validator's vote depends on the size of its deposit or stake. (See Proof of Work and Proof of Authority)

Proof of Work: Proof of Work or POW, is a method that ties mining capability to computational power and secureness of transaction. In the mining system blocks are hashed, which as we mention before, is an easy computational process (as long as you have the proper equipment), so for this process to be more encrypted or protected an additional variable is added to the mix to make it more difficult to replicate or copy so that each transaction is unique and secure. In a sense, we want to create a situation where once we see a state of a ledger and accept it as correct, have the tranquility that this product will be impossible to replicate or make it better. This is what proof of work is.

It's kind of like a cryptographic puzzle or enigma put on purpose to make it more difficult to create blocks and since we can assume that the puzzle is difficult to crack, it is safe to say that it must have taken a lot of time and computational effort to achieve. Thus, a hashed block is considered proof of work. The common proof of work protocol requires that of any two conflicting circumstances we get on the network we must choose the one that was hardest to create. As we mentioned before, the process of Bitcoin mining and solving the POW consumes a lot of computational power and electrical energy. It is estimated that one Bitcoin transaction requires the amount of electrical energy needed to fully power 1.5 American households daily. (See Mining, POA and POS)

Protocols: Protocols are a collection of specific rules that define how to transfer specific data across a particular network or Blockchain.

Pump and Dump: A Pump and Dump is a slang term used to describe a group or entity that promotes and/or invests on an Altcoin, even if they don't actually believe on their technology or purpose, to try to get the price of this specific cryptocurrency to grow, so that when it reaches a profitable quantity selling all their coins of this company and/or crypto to get a massive gain.

Ripple: Ripple is a payment network built on distributed ledgers that can be used to transfer any currency. The network consists of payment nodes and gateways operated by authorities. Ripple provides one frictionless experience to send money globally using the power of Blockchain. By joining Ripple's growing, global network, financial institutions can process their customers' payments anywhere in the world instantly, reliably and cost-effectively. Banks and payment providers can use the digital asset XRP to further reduce their costs and access new markets. Ripple is a technology that acts as both a cryptocurrency and a digital payment network for financial transactions. Ripple operates on an open source and peer to peer decentralized platform that allows for a seamless transfer of money in any form, whether it is USD, Litecoin or Bitcoin. It recently started a partnership with Western Union and with offices in San Francisco, New York, London, Sydney, India, Singapore and Luxembourg, Ripple has more than 100 customers around the world.

Rekt: Rekt is also a misspell and slang terminology meaning "wrecked" that is mostly used to describe a very bad trade or trades causing the fall of all or most of your assets.

Satoshi: A Satoshi is the smallest fraction of a Bitcoin, think of it as the cents of the Bitcoin, many Satoshis make 1BTC, 1000,000,000 Satoshis to be exact. One Satoshi or 0.00000001 BTC, that is, a hundredth of a millionth BTC is the smallest amount of Satoshis you can have.

Satoshi Nakamoto: Satoshi Nakamoto is very difficult to explain. Many will call him, her or it the God of cryptocurrency but I like to think of it as a scientific genius. Satoshi Nakamoto is the name used to describe the person, group or entity that designed the bitcoin protocol and its original implementation in 2009. As part of the implementation, they also devised the first Blockchain database. Many people have speculated about who is the inventor of Bitcoin, but the beauty of the invention is not the inventor but the technology itself. Bitcoin and the Blockchain are to money as cellphones are to telephones, what internet is to libraries, what electricity is to candles and what cars are to carriages, yes we can still use all of them but as time progresses the practicality and functionality of them will increase to the point that we won't be able to live a normal life without using them at least once a week.

(See Blockchain and Bitcoin)

Scammer: For scammers there's not much explanation needed. Scammers are people or groups that trick people into buying, trading or giving cryptocurrency to others in exchange for "massive gains", in my experience, if it's too good to be true, it is too good to be true. Scams often revolve around ICOs and/or investment organizations.

Scrypt: Scrypt is an alternative proof of work system to SHA-256, first introduced with the emergence of Litecoin. This particular algorithm was designed to be user friendly to Central Processing Unit and Graphical Processing Unit miners (CPU and GPU) but with very little advantages to Application Specific Integrated Circuit miners (ASIC). Its advantages include lower block times and less energy consumption.

SHA 256: The (Secure Hash Algorithm) SHA-256 is one of the most common systems used by cryptocurrency miners to authenticate mined blocks of transaction data. This algorithm is put into place by the developers of the cryptocurrency, put into practice by the miners and used by Bitcoin and most of the cryptocurrencies based upon its code.

Data block processing with SHA-256 tends to have slower transaction turnaround times, which for some miners can be a little frustrating but some miners advocate for it stating that it is also more secure and thorough thus leaving less room for error. So basically, an algorithm or a set of rules to be followed in calculations for problem solving operations in a node or computer to create blocks in the Blockchain. (See Scrypt and POW)

Shill: Shill or shilling is the act of deceiving the crypto masses. It basically means to trick as many people as possible into thinking a particular coin or token will increase exponentially in value (moon) in the future to earn profits from it. (See FUD and FOMO)

Shitcoin: A Shitcoin is usually a token or coin that has little to no technology behind it, no real application, untrustworthy and mostly used for pump and dump or to shill. Some of these Shitcoins could be abandoned projects or test platforms that didn't work.

Slang: Type of language that consists of words and phrases that are regarded as very informal or popular. They are mostly used in a particular group or people with the same interest and are more commonly used in speech than writing.

Smart Contracts: Smart Contracts are agreements used in the Blockchain to digitally facilitate and implement the negotiation of an agreement and help people exchange assets such as, currency and shares avoiding a third-party member such as banks or lawyers. It uses a cryptographic code or computer language instead of a legal language.

Softfork: A Softfork is a change to the bitcoin protocol where updated versions of the protocol are backwards compatible with previous versions, meaning that if you were to make a transaction on the old software the new version of the software would be able to recognize the transaction and accepted but transactions made on the new software won't be able to be understood by the new software. This "Softfork" not only permits older versions to recognize the new blocks but also only requires a majority of the miners upgrading to enforce the new rules. Although soft forks can't be reversed without a Hard Fork coming into place it is important to denote that all nodes, even if they have not been updated, will continue to recognize new blocks and maintain consensus on the Blockchain. Think of it as an update to the Bitcoin protocol (where Bitcoin stays Bitcoin) to make either transactions faster, blocks bigger or changes to promote a better mining and smoother transaction exchanges. (See Hardfork)

Source Code Fork: A Source code fork is a classification used for an altcoin that is neither a hard fork nor soft fork. One of the most used and famous altcoins that comply with the requirements to be called a Source Code Forks or forkcoin is Litecoin. To be classified as a soft fork or hard fork, the divergence must share some of the same chain from the genesis block (first block of the Blockchain). Basically, a project that is developed from the idea and protocols of an existing Blockchain but does not share a connection to the Genesis Block of that Blockchain. (See Softfork and Hardfork)

Token: A token is a digital mark of identification for something that can be owned and has some kind of intrinsic value. Contrary to a coin, a token depends on another cryptocurrency as a platform to operate. (See coin and cryptocurrency)

Token-less ledger: A Token-less ledger refers to a distributed ledger that doesn't require an innate or local currency to function.

Transaction block: A Transaction Block is a group of transactions on a specific network, assembled as a block that can be hashed and incorporated to the Blockchain.

Transaction fees: The Transaction fees are small charges imposed on the transactions sent across the network. This transaction fee serves as payment to the miners that successfully hash the block containing the specific transaction.

Total Supply: A Total Supply of a currency is the total amount of coins in existence at the moment, this can change with new blocks being hashed (bitcoins being created) and/or coins being burned (discarding of coins).

Unpermissioned Blockchains: Unpermissioned Blockchains are Blockchains created without an access control layer into their nodes thus allowing everyone in the network to have the capability to take part in the blockchain's network.

Unpermissioned Ledgers: In Cryptocurrency an unpermissioned ledger is a digital record or ledger that allows any actor or node to contribute data to the ledger, this prevents one-sided transactions and fraudulent transactions to be added. Miners maintain the integrity of the ledger by reaching an agreement about its state.

Vitalik Buterin: Vitalik Buterin is the co-creator and face of Ethereum. He first discovered Blockchain and cryptocurrency technologies through Bitcoin in 2011 and was immediately excited by the technology and its potential. He is also the co-creator of Bitcoin Magazine. In 2013 he wrote the Ethereum white paper prompting the creation of a new Blockchain and protocol configuration. He now leads Ethereum's research team, working on future versions of the Ethereum protocol.

Wallet: In the case of Cryptocurrency a Digital Wallet, is a file that contains a collection of private keys. Much like your normal wallet it holds the currency that you possess but with the only difference that you must have a different wallet for each Blockchain currency, for example: if you have Bitcoin, Ethereum and Ripple you must have a wallet for each one. If for some reason you try to transfer a specific currency to a wallet of a different currency the transaction will not be completed and the currency most likely will get lost.

(See Private Keys)

Weak Hands: Weak Hands is a slang term used to describe traders and/or holders that cannot be patient with their cryptocurrency and tend to trade or sell every time they see a dip on the market resulting in profit loss.
(See Buy the Dip and Dip)

Whale: A Whale is a term used to describe a trader or holder that has a substantial amount of cryptocurrency. Whales, with one move, can shake the price and standing of a specific cryptocurrency.

Made in the USA
Monee, IL
04 November 2026

67380166R00030